Literacy in Context

Language to
persuade, argue and advise

Shelagh Hubbard

General editors **Joan Ward** *and* **John O'Connor**
Literacy consultant **Lyn Ranson**
General consultant **Frances Findlay**

PUBLISHED BY THE PRESS SYNDICATE OF THE UNIVERSITY OF CAMBRIDGE
The Pitt Building, Trumpington Street, Cambridge, United Kingdom

CAMBRIDGE UNIVERSITY PRESS
The Edinburgh Building, Cambridge CB2 2RU, UK
40 West 20th Street, New York, NY 10011-4211, USA
10 Stamford Road, Oakleigh, VIC 3166, Australia
Ruiz de Alarcón 13, 28014 Madrid, Spain
Dock House, The Waterfront, Cape Town 8001, South Africa

http://www.cambridge.org

© Cambridge University Press 2001

First published 2001
Second printing 2001

Printed in the United Kingdom at the University Press, Cambridge

Typeface Delima   *System* QuarkXPress®

A catalogue record for this book is available from the British Library

ISBN 0 521 80562 7 paperback

Prepared for publication by Pentacor Plc

Illustrations by Judy Brown (p.9), Adrian Barclay (pp.27, 38, 39), Mark Duffin (pp.32, 33, 62, 63), Paul Hess (p.74)

ACKNOWLEDGEMENTS
The publishers gratefully acknowledge the following for permission to reproduce copyright material.

Textual material Extracts from 'A cold blooded trade', RSPCA leaflet (pp.14, 15), by permission of the RSPCA (Full text of leaflet available on request from: RSPCA HQ, Wilberforce Way, Oakhurst Business Park, Southwater, Horsham, West Sussex RH13 7WN); Eden Project leaflet (pp.20, 21), text and images by permission of The Eden Project and Gendell Design; The *Newspaper* (pp.26, 27), by permission of Young Media Ltd (Web site http://*www.thenewspaper.org.uk*); *Charlie and the Chocolate Factory* (p.39) by Roald Dahl (Penguin Books), by permission of David Higham Associates Ltd.; *eHow* (pp.50, 51) by James M. Hackett (Web site http://*www.eHow.com*), courtesy of *www.eHow.com* copyright © eHow, Inc; 'Living With Asthma' leaflet (pp, 56, 57) by permission of Boots the Chemist; GMTV broadcast (p.62), by permission of GMTV; 'In the Stars' (p.64), by permission of GMTV; 'Life Crisis' (pp. 64, 65) from *Bliss Magazine*, by permission of Bliss Magazine; 'I Have a Dream' (pp.72, 73) from *Strength to Love* by Martin Luther King, Jr. (Hodder and Stoughton), by permission of Laurence Pollinger Ltd. and the estate of Martin Luther King; *Animal Farm* (pp.73, 74) by George Orwell, copyright © George Orwell 1945, by permission of A. M. Heath & Co Ltd. on behalf of Bill Hamilton as the Literary Executor of the Estate of the Late Sonia Brownell Orwell and Martin Secker & Warburg Ltd.; 'Imagine'(p.73) by John Lennon, by permission of Lenono Music.

Photographs Turtle (p.14) ref: REPT 105 © Dave Bevan, by permission of RSPCA Photolibrary; Snake (p.15) ref: REPT 157 © Cheryl A Ertelt, by permission of RSPCA Photolibrary; Children (pp.26, 27) by permission of Young Media; Nicola (p.56) by permission of Boots the Chemist; Martin Luther King (p.73) ref: Black Star F-4915 © Flip Schulke, by permission of Colourific Photo Library Ltd; John Lennon (p.75) ref: 20686, by permission of The Ronald Grant Archive.

Every effort has been made to trace copyright holders, but in some cases this has proved impossible. The publishers would be happy to hear from any copyright holder that has not been acknowledged.

Introduction

- Read a piece of text
- Read it again to discover what makes it special
- Check that you understand it
- Focus on key features
- Learn about the language features and practise using them
- Improve your spelling
- Plan and write your own similar piece
- Check it and redraft

Each unit in this book helps you to understand more about a particular kind of writing, learn about its language features and work towards your own piece of writing in a similar style.

Grammar, spelling and punctuation activities, based on the extract, will improve your language skills and take your writing to a higher level.

 The book at a glance

The texts

The extracts are taken from the National Curriculum reading lists. Each part of the book contains units of extracts and activities at different levels to help you measure your progress.

Each unit includes these sections:

Purpose

This explains exactly what you will read, learn about and write.

Key features

These are the main points to note about the way the extract is written.

Language skills

These activities will improve your grammar, punctuation and spelling. They are all based on the extracts. They are organised using the Word, Sentence and Text Level Objectives of the *National Literacy Strategy Framework*.

Planning your own writing

This structured, step-by-step guide will help you to get started, use writing frames and then redraft and improve your work.

Teacher's Portfolio

This includes worksheets for more language practice, revision and homework. Self-assessment charts will help you to judge and record what level you have reached and to set your own targets for improvement.

Contents

Word	Spelling	Sentence	Text	Activities
• Contracted words and apostrophes	• Homophones of contracted words	• Syntax to emphasise: adverbs, auxiliary verb *do*	• First-person viewpoint • Informal style	Write a letter apologising for a misdemeanour
• Specialist terms • Compound words • Play on words	• add *-ed*	• Active and passive verbs	• Selection • Repetition • Appeals to reader	Write a case study for a campaign leaflet
• Neologism and word roots	• Hard and soft *g*	• Adjectives • Lists of adjectives and nouns	• Text and image	Create advertising leaflet for a tourist attraction.

• Synonyms	• Silent letters: *wr-*, *-ight*	• Commas	• Selecting evidence: facts/opinions	Write a newspaper article giving conflicting points of view
• Emotive words	• Unusual plurals: *-y* /*-ies*	• Sentence types: statement, rhetorical question, imperative	• Structure of argument	Write a letter to newspaper
• Rhetoric in choice of words: irony, exaggeration	• Unstressed vowels: *-l*	• Colons and semicolons in lists	• Bias and selection of arguments • Paragraph links and connectives	Write a formal debate speech

Contents

Word	Spelling	Sentence	Text	Activities
• Imperatives	• -ing participles	• Simple and complex sentences • Conjunctions	• Personal/impersonal tone • Structure: lists	Write an advisory code
• Imperative verbs	• American spelling: practice/ practise	• Clauses • Simple, compound and complex sentences • Commas	• Text organisation: icons, sub-headings, lists, numbers, bullet points	Make a contribution to eHow Web site
• Jargon • Noun phrases	• Word families and letter strings from ancient Greek	• Simple and complex sentences • Clauses • Commas	• First-person viewpoint/ second-person audience • Structure: sections	Create a leaflet of advice on a health issue

Word	Spelling	Sentence	Text	Activities
• Time adverbials	• -ould	• Verb tenses • Auxiliary verbs • Modal verbs	• First, second and third person • Direct address to second-person audience • Colloquial style • Specialist vocabulary	Put together the text for a magazine page: two media texts giving advice about the future
• Antonyms	• Abstract noun suffixes: -ty, -ity	• Rhetorical devices: repetition, rule of three • Simple sentences	• Beginnings and endings	Write a rhetorical speech

Apologies!

In this unit you will:
- read a letter of apology
- learn about persuasive language
- write your own letter saying sorry

▶▶ **Subject links:** *PSHE, drama*

2 ▶ **Letter of apology**

A letter to Miss Richell

What Jenna wrote:

Dear Miss Richell

I know I have apologised so many times, but this time I mean it. I want to say 'sorry' for all the things I have done wrong.

Friday afternoon was a disaster. I know I shouldn't talk during the register, but Debbie was saying things about me. I ignored you when you said 'be quiet' and I was mumbling under my breath when you told me off.

It was Debbie's fault I was in a bad mood. We had an argument at dinner time so it's not fair on you. I'm really very, very sorry. You're right to say I deserved a detention because I shouldn't have argued with you. I really do apologise for swearing. I know that is wrong.

Mr Watson warned me that I'd have to go to Ms. Steel instead of tutor room for registration if I do it again and I don't really want to. The thing is, I know I've got to buck my ideas up before it's too late. I do like this school and I do want to stay in your tutor group.

I'm so sorry I don't know how to say it. The problem is I'm already in detention on Tuesday for History and Mr Patel will give me an hour if I don't go this week. So please will you give me some extra work to do and I'll bring it to you tomorrow morning.

Will you accept this apology from me?

From Jenna
(The one in your tutor group)
P.S. Keep this letter to yourself.

What Jenna said:

Soz Miss ...
didn't mean to talk ... Debs was calling
me and I was mad ... please let me off the det.
Miss ... I'm already in loads of trouble with Sir and
he'll go ballistic if I don't ... I'll do extra work
Miss ... sorry I swore Miss ... I'll be good next
week ... promise Miss.

3 ▶ Key features

The writer:

- repeats how sorry she is, using adverbs and the auxiliary verb *do* for emphasis

- includes sentences that state clear reasons for her behaviour

- writes in a personal, informal style

- Who wrote this letter to whom?
  What had happened?
- What is the letter writer trying to persuade the reader to do?
- Whose side are you on after reading this letter? Why?

4 > Language skills

Word

When we speak, we say words quickly and shorten them. In informal writing, we copy speech by missing letters out of some words. We call these 'contracted words'.

The **apostrophe** (') is a punctuation mark with two quite different uses. One use is to show where a letter or a group of letters has been missed out of contracted words.

This letter's style is chatty and personal. It has quite a few contracted words: *it's* is a short way of writing *it is* or *it has*.

❶ These examples are taken from Jenna's letter. Write them down with the apostrophes in the correct places. Check the letter to see if you were right.

> *I shouldnt talk*
>
> *I dont really want to*
>
> *Youre right*
>
> *Im so sorry*
>
> *Ill bring it to you*
>
> *Ive got to buck my ideas up before its too late*

❷ Make two columns. In the left-hand column, list all the contracted words in Jenna's letter. In the right-hand column, write the words in full, with the missing letters replaced.

Spelling

Homophones are words which sound the same, but have a different spelling and meaning.

Contracted words often cause spelling problems because they are easily confused with other words that sound the same: *they're* and *there*, *you're* and *your*.

One way to check which is the correct spelling is to say the sentence with the contracted words in full. If it makes sense, you need the spelling with the apostrophe.

❶ Write these sentences with the correct spelling of the homophone.

> *I think (there/they're) very sorry now.*
>
> *That is (your/you're) coat.*
>
> *(Their/They're) silly behaviour has caused all this trouble.*
>
> *(Its/It's) about time you grew up.*
>
> *What (your/you're) saying now is a lie.*
>
> *That car needs (its/it's) windows cleaning.*

Sentence

Adverbs are words which give more information about a verb, an adjective or another adverb.

She spoke **apologetically**.
(Verb and adverb)

She spoke **quite** *apologetically*.
(adverb and adverb)

She was **rather** *apologetic*. (adverb and adjective)

In persuasive writing you can add certain words to sentences to emphasise a point. Some adverbs are used with an adjective for this reason.

I'm **so** *sorry. I'm* **really very** *sorry*.

These adverbs can add emphasis: *very, so, most, completely, definitely, absolutely, truly, unquestionably, categorically*.

❶ Add different adverbs to these sentences to emphasise the point that is being made.

I know that swearing is .... wrong.

You're .... right to say I deserved a detention.

It's .... not fair on you.

❷ Write down the most persuasive version of each sentence you have created.

An **auxiliary verb** is a verb form we put before the main verb to change its meaning.

Jenna's letter shows how you can use the auxiliary verb *do* for emphasis, like this:

I **do** *like this school.* (Auxiliary verb *do* emphasises main verb, *like*.)

Text

When we write something from our own viewpoint, using the **pronoun** *I*, we call this writing in the **first person**: *I apologise, I mean it, I will do extra work.*

When we write in a personal style, we write in the first person.

❶ Note down three sentences where Jenna uses the first-person pronoun *I* to say 'sorry' to her tutor.

The **audience** is the name we give to the people we expect will read our writing or listen to what we say. A letter like this is written to one particular person, so we use the **second-person pronoun**, *you*, as if we were talking directly to our audience:

You're right to say I deserved a detention..., it's not fair on you...

❷ Note down two sentences from paragraphs two and three where Jenna admits how she has behaved badly to her tutor, using the pronoun *you*.

❸ Note down one sentence where Jenna asks her tutor a direct question.

5 > Planning your own writing

Write your own letter to someone you know well. Apologise for something you have done, and persuade them to change their mind about punishing you.

≫ STARTING POINTS

- You borrowed a computer game and lost it. Your friend wants the money to buy a new one – now.
- You have been late home three nights on the run. You have been grounded for the week.
- You broke a window while you were playing football. Until you pay for it, you cannot have your football back.
- You haven't done your English homework again. Your teacher has threatened to phone home.
- Or write a letter to apologise for something that you have really done.

≫ CLUES FOR SUCCESS

- Begin by saying 'sorry' ... and keep on saying it!
- Keep the tone personal and informal.
- Use first-person pronoun *I* and second-person pronoun *you* to ask questions.
- Make it clear you know exactly what you have done wrong – confess.
- Give good reasons for your wrong-doing – make an excuse.
- Agree that your reader is right.
- Finally, beg for a different punishment.

≫ REDRAFTING AND IMPROVING

In pairs, read each other's letters and suggest improvements. See if you can:

- make the tone of the letter more personal
- apologise even more often
- add new reasons or explanations
- change words or sentence structures to make points more persuasive
- correct spelling mistakes
- correct punctuation – especially apostrophes

WRITING FRAME

This might help you organise your ideas in paragraphs.

Section	Possible phrases	Language features
Apology Begin by saying 'sorry' **Confession** Admit what you have done wrong.	*Dear ...* *I am truly sorry ...* *It was entirely my fault that ...* *I was so wrong when I ...* *It's unfair to you ...* *I do know I shouldn't have ...*	● adverbs and *do* used for emphasis ● informal, personal style ● first- and second-person pronouns ● contracted words with apostrophes
Excuses State reasons to explain your wrongdoing.	*It was completely accidental ...* *It was not entirely my fault ...* *The blame lies more with ...*	● blame a third person
Praise Explain the reasons why your reader is right, and is important to you.	*You were absolutely correct ...* *I understand why you were so angry ...* *You are always completely fair ...*	● adverbs for emphasis ● second-person pronouns
Beg Ask for forgiveness and a different punishment.	*I beg you to ...* *Please would you ...* *Will you ...*	● direct questions ● indirect requests

6 ▷ Looking back

- **Apostrophes** replace missing letters in contracted words. They are used when you write in an informal style that sounds like speech.

- **Adverbs** such as *really* and *very* and the **auxiliary verb** *do* may be added to a sentence to emphasise important ideas.

- **First person** is when you write as *I*. Use it when you want to write to your audience in a personal style.

Cruelty campaign

1 ▷ Purpose

In this unit you will:

- read a charity leaflet campaigning against exotic pets
- learn how language and pictures persuade you to support the campaign
- write your own persuasive case study

≫ **Subject links:** *science, geography, PSHE*

2 ▷ RSPCA leaflet persuading you to take action

A cold-blooded trade

These are extracts from a leaflet to persuade people to join the campaign to limit trade in exotic pets. 'Exotic' means unusual, wild animals such as lizards, snakes, spiders and birds.

RSPCA Information

A cold-blooded trade –

Think again if you want an exotic pet

Wild warning!

Every year, millions of wild animals are trapped for use in the exotic pet trade – most die before reaching pet shops and many species are now endangered because of the trade.

Wild-caught animals
– what are their chances of survival?

- Some die at the time of capture – methods can be cruel and inappropriate.
- More die because they don't have time to recover from the trauma of capture.
- More die due to bad transport and depot-holding conditions in exporting countries.
- More die when they are badly packaged and despatched overseas, mainly by air.
- More die when they get to pet shops – they need to rest, recover and acclimatise.

Think about the cost...

Abandoned lizard

The RSPCA rescued a badly-neglected lizard from a house whose owner had moved away leaving it without proper care. The lizard had an infection which was so severe it could no longer move. The lizard was put to sleep to end its suffering.

Python problem

A man with no knowledge of how to care for snakes tried to keep a 12ft Burmese python that was dumped on his doorstep. He fed it chicken, let it sleep in his bed and turned his heating right up before calling the RSPCA. The Society has found a suitable home for the snake.

Snapping turtle

A vicious snapping turtle had to be rescued from a London park after jamming itself under the wheel of a police patrol car. It had probably been abandoned after it grew to about 50cm (20 ins) long and 9kg (20lbs) in weight, and became too much for its owner.

Don't buy an exotic animal without knowing what you're really in for ...

- How long will it live?
- How big will it grow?
- How much space will it need?

Call for action

- Urge your local council to set strict licensing standards for pet shops including compulsory written welfare information and annual visits by an experienced vet. Ask it to end exotic trade events.
- Register your opposition to the trade in wild-caught animals with your MP and local council.

Cruelty watch

If you see an animal which you believe is suffering unnecessarily, please call the RSPCA's cruelty line on ...

---

3 ❯ **Key features**

The leaflet:

- uses repetition to emphasise cruelty and suffering
- selects information to influence the reader's opinion
- instructs the reader on how to take action to support the campaign

---

- List five ways exotic animals suffer and three actions you can take to stop this.
- Do pet shops look after exotic animals well, judging from this leaflet?
- What does the leaflet tell you about the good side of owning an exotic pet?

4 ▷ Language skills

Word

Writers often have to use **specialist words** when they write about a particular topic.

❶ Here are some of the specialist words used in the leaflet. Use each one in a sentence of your own.

> *exotic (foreign, unusual, colourful)*
>
> *trauma (shock, pain)*
>
> *despatched (sent, posted)*
>
> *endangered (in danger of dying out)*

A **play on words** is the use of a word with more than one meaning, often to get a humorous effect. Newspaper headlines are a good place to look out for these.

❷ The title of this leaflet is 'A cold-blooded trade'. Write definitions of the two different meanings of *cold-blooded* which make this a clever play on words.

A **compound word** is two words joined into one, like *blackbird*. Some compound words are joined with a hyphen, like *bad-tempered*.

❸ *Cold-blooded* is a compound word. Find another compound word in the text. It is an important word in this leaflet, but it is not in the dictionary. Write your own definition of its meaning.

Spelling

❶ Look carefully at the ways in which a verb's spelling changes when it is put into the passive or the past tense. Copy out the chart and add at least two examples of your own for each spelling rule. The text will start you off, then use a dictionary if you need to.

Root words	Examples	Spelling rule
Regular verbs	dump ➜ dump**ed** abandon ➜ abandon**ed**	Add *-ed*.
Verbs ending with *-e*	rescue ➜ rescue**d** move ➜ move**d**	Add *-d*.
Verbs ending with *-y*	try ➜ tr**ied** deny ➜ den**ied**	Change the *y* to *i* and add *-ed*.
Verbs with 'short' vowel sounds	jam ➜ jam**med** trap ➜ trap**ped**	Double the last letter and add *-ed*.

Sentence

There are two ways of describing an action. If we use the **active** form of the verb, we focus on the person who is doing the action:

The RSPCA rescued a lizard ...

The RSPCA is the subject of the sentence.

❶ Write down another sentence with an active verb form where the RSPCA is the subject of the sentence.

If we use the **passive** form, we focus more on the action.

> A vicious snapping turtle **had to be rescued** from a London park ...

We don't actually know who the rescuer was, so the animal's suffering is drawn to our attention.

2 Write down two sentences where passive verbs focus your attention on the harm and suffering of animals. Underline the passive verb forms.

3 Who caused the suffering? Is it mentioned in the sentences, or did you have to work it out for yourself? Note down your answer.

Text

Many persuasive techniques are used in this leaflet. All the way through, the words and the pictures are **selected** carefully to influence your opinion and your actions.

Repetition of key words is used for emphasis.

1 In this text, certain words are repeated to emphasise animals' suffering. Write down two sentences where each of these words is used: *cruel/cruelty, bad/badly*

2 Repetition is used to answer the question, *What are their chances of survival?* Write down the repeated words. How many times are these words repeated?

Case studies give real-life examples of the problem to persuade you that it happens frequently.

3 In this leaflet, there are three, detailed case studies of cruelty to exotic pets. Read the case studies and write down at least four words or phrases used to show people's ignorance about looking after exotic animals.

4 Write down at least four words and phrases which show the harm done to the three animals.

Persuasive techniques include **appeals** to you, which can be **imperatives** (commands) or **questions**.

This leaflet persuades you, personally, to do something about the problem of cruelty to exotic pets.

Register your opposition ... (an imperative)

How big will it grow? (a question you need to ask yourself before you buy)

5 Read all the parts of the leaflet that appeal to you to take action. Write down four imperatives that tell you to do something.

Write down two questions the leaflet says you should ask before you buy an exotic pet.

5 ❭ Planning your own writing

Write your own case study to persuade readers to support a charity of your choice.

❭❭ STARTING POINTS

Persuade your readers by shocking them with a description of pain and suffering. Make your readers feel sympathy with a positive account of how your charity changed someone's life.

Decide what sort of charity you will write about then think about a case study to base your appeal on. You could choose:

- another example of ignorance leading to suffering, or the death, of an exotic pet

- people suffering in a country affected by a disaster such as flood, war or famine

- a person who became homeless – and how your charity has helped

- a child in a developing country who has been helped by food, medicines or education provided by your charity

❭❭ CLUES FOR SUCCESS

- Choose a good title: something short and eye-catching – maybe a play on words, or a question.

- Use passive verbs to focus attention on victims of suffering.

- Use repetition of ideas and important words to emphasise your main points.

- Include detailed facts (numbers, names, places) to make your case study sound real.

WRITING FRAME

Section	Possible phrases *Third person*	*First person*	Language features
The problem	*Four Vietnamese pot-bellied pigs were being kept in a small, twelfth-floor flat ...*	*I answered an emergency call to a block of flats where four pot-bellied pigs were held captive ...*	● facts and figures ● passive verbs
The suffering	*The pigs were in a terrible state ...*	*I was appalled by what I saw ...*	● words and phrases repeatedly emphasising cruelty and suffering
The action taken	*The pigs were taken to safety in a city farm ...*	*We acted swiftly: the pigs were rehomed ...*	● passive verbs focusing on the victims
The outcome	*Three pigs are now happily settled. Sadly, one was so ill that ...*	*A week later I visited the farm. The pigs were transformed. It was wonderful ...*	● words emphasising happy (or sad) results

 REDRAFTING AND IMPROVING

Discuss your case studies in pairs and suggest ways to improve them. Check whether you can:

● add more details, facts or figures to make your case study more realistic

● include repetition of a word, a phrase, or an idea to emphasise an important point

● change verbs from active to passive to focus attention on the suffering of the victims

6 ▷ Looking back

● **Passive verbs** focus attention on a suffering victim.

● **Repetition** emphasises main points or important ideas.

● **Selection** of information – both words and pictures – persuades your reader to support you.

The big build

1 > ## Purpose

In this unit you will:

- read a leaflet advertising a new tourist attraction
- learn how language and pictures persuade you to visit the Eden Project
- write your own advertisement for a tourist attraction

>> **Subject links:** *citizenship, science, geography*

2 > ## Advertisement for the Eden Project

The big build

The world's best kept secret is revealed May 15th – November 5th 2000

the
big
build

eden project

www.edenproject.com

See history in the making

The 8th wonder of the world will open fully in Spring 2001 ...

...but so great has been the demand for previews that there will be a chance, for a limited period, to actually go behind the scenes and see the big build in progress.

Space age technology meets the lost world in the giant 50 metre deep crater. The size of 35 football pitches, it is being sculpted to make a living theatre of plants and people – a global garden that will be ready for planting late in summer 2000.

Nestling within it are two gigantic geodesic conservatories – the largest in the world. Made from over 800 huge steel hexagons with no internal support, they are a remarkable feat of engineering.

Come to the Eden Project before full opening and look down upon all this construction at first hand from The Gallery in our Visitor Centre. There you'll also find a multi-media presentation of 'The making of Eden' – bringing to life all the architectural, horticultural and construction challenges we've met along the way.

There's a coffee bar and a shop selling a range of limited edition Eden merchandise from clothing to stationery, from Fair Trade coffee and chocolate to a range of special Eden plants.

And, looking forward to the full opening in 2001, a unique exhibition previews our ambitious plans for the future at this epic location.

You'll have to wait another year to be able to walk through the 'biomes' and experience the sights, smells and sheer scale of the rainforest but for the limited period from May 15th to November 5th, 2000 why not grab a sneak preview of Eden in the making – before the rest of the world discovers us?

Eden opens fully in 2001. But you can see it under construction this summer.

Our mission: to promote the understanding and practise the responsible management of the vital relationship between plants, people and resources, leading towards a sustainable future for all.

Open 10am – 6pm every day

Last entry 5pm

May 15th – Nov 5th 2000

A MILLENNIUM PROJECT

SUPPORTED BY FUNDS FROM THE EUROPEAN DEVELOPMENT FUND

The Visitor Centre

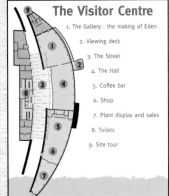

1. The Gallery - the making of Eden
2. Viewing deck
3. The Street
4. The Hall
5. Coffee bar
6. Shop
7. Plant display and sales
8. Toilets
9. Site tour

3 ▷ Key features

The writers of the leaflet:

- combine language and images to make the Eden Project sound exciting
- use adjectives to emphasise the size of the project
- write in a style with many conversational features

- What is the Eden Project and where is it?
- When was it completed, and why might visitors have been interested to see it before then?
- What is the main attraction of the Eden Project that visitors in 2000 did not see?

4 Language skills

Word

Newly invented words are sometimes called **neologisms**. New words are often made by combining words whose roots come from ancient Greek or Latin. The word *neologism* is a nineteenth-century example. It has two root words: *neos* which is Greek for *new* and *logos* which is Greek for *word*.

Many subjects you learn at school got their names in the same way. *Biology* comes from *logos* (literally, 'words about') and *bio-* (life). Geology comes from *logos* and geo- (earth).

❶ What is a *geodesic* conservatory? Where on the leaflet is there a picture of one? Write down the sentences in the text which describe it.

❷ Note down your explanation of the root word of *geodesic*. How is the root word (*geo-*) linked with the name of a geodesic dome?

❸ *Biome* is a new noun. Write down what the leaflet says about it. How does the leaflet show that it is a neologism? Note down what you think about the root (*bio-*) of this word. Then write a brief definition, with a sketch copied from the leaflet to show what one looks like.

Spelling

In English the same letter can represent more than one sound. The letter *g* is an example: it can have a **hard** sound as it has in *global garden*, but sometimes it has a **soft** sound as it has in the words *giant* and *geodesic*.

❶ Copy these lists of words from the leaflet. Add at least two more words to each list.

Hard *g*: *global, garden, gallery, great, progress, hexagon*

Soft *g*: *geodesic, giant, engineer, challenge, largest*

Sentence

Adjectives are words used to describe someone or something. They give more information about a noun or a pronoun. In the phrase *global garden*, the adjective *global* describes the noun *garden*.

In advertisements, adjectives are an important part of persuasive language.

❶ List the adjectives in these sentences which emphasise the scale of this project.

See the big build in progress.

They are a remarkable feat of engineering.

A unique exhibition previews our ambitious plans for the future at this epic location.

2 The adjective *limited* is repeated. Copy out three phrases where this word is used.

3 *For a limited period* ... emphasises that there is not much time to see the project before it is finished. Note down how the other uses of *limited* add to the idea that a visit to the project would be a very special experience.

4 How does the adjective in *sneak preview* add to the idea that visits in the summer of 2000 are special? Note down your explanation.

Lists of adjectives or nouns emphasise how special something is. In this extract, lists build up the idea of the great size of the project and the technical achievement.

5 Copy out these phrases and underline the adjectives. How do they suggest that the project is exciting?

The giant 50 metre deep crater ...

Made from over 800 huge steel hexagons ...

... bringing to life all the architectural, horticultural and construction challenges...

6 Copy out these phrases and underline the nouns. How do they persuade you that the project is interesting?

... a living theatre of plants and people – a global garden ...

... the vital relationship between plants, people and resources ...

Text

Advertisers use a combination of **text and images** to persuade you to buy the product.

1 The 'artist's impression' of the completed project is eye-catching. Note down five details it shows you. Explain how this sketch connects with the name, *Eden Project*.

2 Sketch two symbols included in the design of the leaflet and note down what each one means.

3 Which two colours are most noticeable in the design of the leaflet? Note down an explanation of why they have been chosen.

5 ▶ Planning your own writing

Write an advertising leaflet to persuade tourists to visit an attraction in your own area.

▶▶ STARTING POINTS

Your attraction could be real or imagined. It could be:

- a theme park – to appeal either to families or to your own age group
- a famous building – a stately home, a religious site, an ancient monument
- a zoo, wildlife sanctuary or safari park
- something humorous – a gnome reserve, a farm for racing snails, a 'school safari park' with wild pupils in their natural habitat ...

▶▶ CLUES FOR SUCCESS

- Invent a good title for the leaflet: something short and intriguing. Make up an interesting name for your attraction.
- Concentrate on the text first. You can add colour and images later.
- Choose (or neologise) appropriate vocabulary.
- Make good use of adjectives to emphasise how thrilling / unusual / beautiful your attraction is.
- Repetition is persuasive: use lists of adjectives and nouns to emphasise your main points.
- Involve your readers – persuade with a chatty, colloquial style.

▶▶ REDRAFTING AND IMPROVING

Show your advert to a friend. Discuss how you can make improvements.

- Check the title of the leaflet and the names of the attractions.
- Add more, and better, adjectives.
- Use lists of nouns and adjectives for emphasis.
- Colloquial style: make sure you involve your reader with commands and questions.
- If you can use a computer for your final version, you may find a ready-made style sheet for an A4 leaflet. Include images and use colour to help sell your attraction to tourists.

>> WRITING FRAME

Section	Possible phrases or content	Language features
Title and name of attraction	*Mountains of Millennium Fun* *The Alpine Adventure*	● short and catchy ● play on words: *Alps, mountains,* etc ● alliteration
Describe the place	*How high dare you go?* *Experience the thrills of some of the highest rides outside Florida ...*	● direct colloquial style ● adjectives — in lists
Give details about things to see and do	*Ride the Avalanche, for a terrifying, once-in-a-lifetime ...* *Hold tight for an exhilarating blast on the Toboggan Run ...*	● imperatives ● exciting adjectives
Extra activities	*Sit and enjoy refreshments in The Lodge ...* *Visit the shop to buy a range of special woollen goods ...*	● contrasting vocabulary — appeal to a different kind of visitor
Factual information	Directions — opening times — prices — phone — Web site — sponsors —as seen on TV — wheelchair access — dogs permitted, etc.	● short, clear sentences or lists in note form

6 > Looking back

- **Neologisms** are new words invented to name or describe new things.
- **Adjectives** describe nouns. They are carefully chosen to make advertisements persuasive.
- A combination of **text and images** persuades you to buy a product.

For and against

In this unit you will:
- read different opinions written in a newspaper
- learn about language used to write arguments
- write your own newspaper page

➤➤ **Subject links:** *PHSE, citizenship, ICT*

2 ▷ **Newspaper article**

Arguments to state an opinion

IS CANING WRONG?

State schools in the UK no longer cane or smack pupils to punish them. The Newspaper would never be in favour of hitting pupils in school for any reason, but what are the alternatives and do they work?

JOANNA WALLIS MURDOCH dislikes the idea of punishing:
I think we should be able to tell our parents and teachers the reason for our behaviour, what is wrong and what we think should be done about it! Otherwise when we grow up the world will be full of people who have locked up their feelings and can't talk about things that matter to them.

VIRRAJ NAINA is not sure that his school has got it right yet:
I think in my school they are too soft. We have this thing called the 'time penalty' of 20 minutes and three of them give you a detention for an hour after school on Tuesdays. After four weeks, if you have only

one or two 'time penalties', they get crossed off. Even after detention everybody still mucks around.

<small>CHEE FUNG LEE</small> is very sure that caning and beating are wrong, but does believe in punishments:

At school I think the cane should not be brought back because it can cause young people to hate their teachers. As this hatred builds up it will affect how they feel about going to school and carrying on with their education. We have detentions for punishments. These involve wrong-doers sitting in a room doing nothing but writing a really long poem, which is extremely boring and some can do one hour of detention every day of the week. Sometimes you have to help the school keeper pick up rubbish from the school site in break and in lunch-time.

<small>SUZANNAH MALONEY</small> thinks praising is better:
At our school, one of our rewards is Student of the Week, which is handed out in assembly to pupils who have been a pleasure to teach, have done some really good work or have sorted out their behaviour. You can also get stickers on a Friday if you have been on time every day. The best is a letter sent home to say you have been an excellent pupil. If you get any of these rewards, you go into the Golden Book.

3 ▸ Key features

The article:
- gives a variety of conflicting points of view
- explains the reasons for the points of view
- includes both facts and opinions as evidence for points of view

- Why is the headline misleading?
- What is the argument really about? Write the question in your own words, as clearly and simply as you can.
- There are two opposite points of view here. Who is in favour of strict punishments? Who thinks there are better ways of improving behaviour?

4 ⟩ Language skills

Word

A **synonym** is a word which means the same, or almost the same as another word.

At the beginning of the article, the verbs *smack* and *hit* are synonyms.

1 Write down the two synonyms for *hit* in this sentence.

> *Chee Fung Lee is very sure that caning and beating are wrong, but does believe in punishments.*

2 Use a thesaurus to list at least five more synonyms for *hit*. Begin by looking up all four words you already have. Make sure that all your words have the same meaning of *hit* as it is used in this article.

3 The children who gave their opinions nearly all began by saying *I think*. Use your thesaurus to list at least three synonyms for *think*.

Spelling

When you write any argument, you will probably use the words *right* and *wrong*. These words have spellings which are not **phonetic**: the letters do not reflect the sound of the word. Both words have **silent letters** which are not pronounced. In the word *right*, *-ight* sounds like *-ite* and the *gh* is silent. In *wrong*, the *w* is also silent: the word sounds as if it begins with letter *r*.

1 List five other words with the *-ight* ending. Write a sentence for each word to show you understand what it means.

A **mnemonic** is a memorable phrase which helps you to remember something. A **letter string** is a sequence of letters we often find together in the spelling of English words.

A good way to remember letter strings is to make up a silly sentence whose words begin with those letters, for example: *ight – I've Got Horrible Teeth*.

2 Make up your own mnemonic to remember the *-ight* letter string.

3 List six words to show other sounds the *gh* letter string can make, starting with the words *cough*, *ghost* and *bough*.

Sentence

People are more likely to listen to your opinions if you back them up with reasons. Punctuate your statements carefully to separate opinions.

Commas are used to break up long sentences. They have three main uses:

1 IN *WH* CLAUSES

If you make a point and then comment on it, a comma divides the point from the comment.

The punishment is writing out a long poem, which is extremely boring.

Wh clauses like this begin with a *wh-* word such as *who, whom* or *which*. They need a comma to separate them from the rest of the sentence.

2 IN LISTS

Commas separate items in a list.

Rewards are given to pupils who have made an effort, done good work, been helpful or behaved better.

3 AS BRACKETS

Commas go on either side of an extra phrase or clause in the middle of a sentence.

After a week, if you only get one, the time penalty is crossed off.

1 This sentence needs commas. Write it out, correctly punctuated.

I think we should be able to tell our parents and teachers the reason for our behaviour what is wrong and what we think should be done.

Text

When we argue we give reasons. Some of these are **facts** and some are our personal **opinions**. Both help convince other people that we are correct.

A fact is something we know for certain has happened or is true.

Opinions are our own beliefs. They are neither true nor false, but can be backed up with reasons.

Chewing gum should be banned in school because it makes a mess.

1 Here are some quotes from the newspaper article. Write them down in two columns, with headings **Facts** and **Opinions**.

We have detention for punishments.

I think in my school they are too soft.

These involve ... writing a really long poem, which is extremely boring.

... you have to help the school keeper pick up rubbish from the school site.

You can also get stickers on a Friday if you have been on time.

I think the cane should not be brought back ...

2 Sometimes there are clues to when someone is expressing an opinion. Look out for phrases such as *I think ...*, or *I believe that ...*, or *It seems to me ...* Look carefully at the sentences on your list of opinions. Underline the words that tell you it is an opinion, not a fact.

5 ▷ Planning your own writing

Find a topic about which your class has strong opinions. Write your own newspaper article. Include four people's contrasting points of view.

⟫ STARTING POINTS

- Does homework help pupils make better progress?
- Are single-sex schools better than mixed schools?
- Is school uniform a good thing?
- Are school holidays too long?

⟫ CLUES FOR SUCCESS

- You need a headline: an eye-catching question.
- Begin with a short introduction to explain the different sides of the argument.
- Introduce each person's point of view clearly, followed by a colon before you quote their words.
- Give good, detailed reasons for each point of view – a mixture of facts and opinions.
- Make sure you have contrasting points of view and a variety of reasons, for and against.
- Use commas correctly – as brackets and to punctuate *wh* clauses and lists.

⟫ REDRAFTING AND IMPROVING

Read your article carefully and check to see whether you can improve on:

- getting readers interested in the topic: make the headline or introduction more punchy
- backing up the points of view: add new reasons, facts or opinions
- variety of vocabulary: find good synonyms in a thesaurus
- spelling: correct your mistakes, especially missed silent letters
- punctuation, especially commas in longer sentences

>> **WRITING FRAMES**

Use these ideas if you need help to organise your arguments.

Sections	Possible phrases		Language features
	For	**Against**	
Headline and introduction	*Is ... right?* *Should ... be allowed?*	*Is ... wrong?* *Should ... be stopped?*	• questions • Spelling – silent letters *w* and *gh*
The interview Give names and each point of view.	*(Name) agrees entirely that ... :* *(Name) is very sure that ... :*	*(Name) dislikes the idea of ... :* *(Name) is concerned about ... :*	• clear statement of point of view – followed by a colon and their actual words
Arguments Explain the reasons for at least four contrasting points of view.	*I think that ...* *It is right to say ...* *Moreover ...* *Of course ...* *Sometimes ...*	*I disagree because ...* *It is wrong that ...* *Even if ...* *Otherwise ...* *However ...*	• reasons include facts and opinions • varied vocabulary – use of synonyms • varied sentence structures – use of commas

6 > Looking back

- **Synonyms** are words with the same, or almost the same, meaning. Writers use synonyms to make their vocabulary more varied and interesting.

- **Commas** break up sentences and make them easier to understand. They are used in *wh* clauses, in lists and as brackets.

- **Facts** and **opinions** are different: a fact is something we know for certain; an opinion is someone's personal belief. Both can be used as evidence for your point of view.

From my point of view

1 ▶ **Purpose**

In this unit you will:
- read a letter to the newspaper
- learn about language used to write a convincing argument
- write your own letter arguing for or against a point of view

▶▶ **Subject links:** *citizenship, PSHE*

2 ▶ **Letter to the editor**

In defence of teenagers

I am very angry about the number of letters which have appeared in The Evening Post recently, criticising young people in Newton. In particular, I object to the letter from Old Soldier (Letters page, November 5th) where he claimed that today's teenagers are all selfish, uncaring vandals.

He is wrong to judge all of us just because he has seen a few people behaving badly in the shopping precinct. The majority of teenagers are concerned about the environment and would not dream of damaging their own town in that way. Has he never noticed that a group of more than thirty volunteers from my school regularly weed the flower beds, remove graffiti and clear up litter in the park near the shopping centre?

Selfish and uncaring we are not! My school does a great deal of work for charity. Last year we collected well over £1,000. We also had a speaker from Age Concern and now almost a quarter of my year group visit senior citizens in the area. Many of these people are in their seventies and eighties so they appreciate help from their young friends with heavy shopping and with chores around the house. Just ask these older people if all teenagers are selfish!

I hope this letter convinces your readers that most young people are caring and responsible, because that is the truth!

Young environmentalist

3 Key features

The writer:

- uses emotive words to persuade readers
- includes sentences that make statements, give commands and ask rhetorical questions
- organises the argument in short clear paragraphs

» ● Who has written this letter, and why?
● Where would you expect to read it?
● There are two opposite points of view here. What are they? Who is arguing with whom?

4 ▷ Language skills

Word

Writers use **emotive words** when they want to have a particular effect on our feelings and emotions.

Negative emotive words make us feel unpleasant emotions: anger, disgust or shock. *Filthy dustbin*, to describe a town centre, encourages us to share anger and disgust about litter.

Positive emotive words make us feel pleasant emotions: pleased, happy or impressed.

An oasis of calm, to describe a town centre, encourages us to feel pleased about banning traffic and planting flower beds.

❶ The letter from 'Old Soldier' described teenagers with three negative emotive words. He used two adjectives: *selfish* and *uncaring*. He used one noun: *vandals*. Note down these words and explain what they persuade readers to feel about teenagers.

❷ The letter from 'Young environmentalist' argues back with positive emotive words – the very opposite of Old Soldier's.

- An adjective which describes teenagers in a positive way is *caring*. Note down one more.

- A noun with a positive effect is *environmentalist*. Note down two more.

- A verb which shows teenagers do good deeds is *help*. Note down two more.

Spelling

The most common way of turning a noun into its **plural** is to add -*s*: *teenagers; senior citizens*.

❶ List five other plural words from the letter which just add -*s*.

❷ The letter also has some examples of words with different plural spellings. From the letter, write down the plurals of *seventy* and *eighty*. List three other words in the letter, also ending in -*y*, which have plural spellings with the same pattern.

❸ Write a rule to explain how nouns ending with -*y* are made into plurals.

Sentence

A statement is a sentence that states a fact or an opinion:

My friends give money to charity (a fact)

My friends are very kind (my opinion)

❶ It is important in any argument to make clear statements which get your point of view across, for example *My school does a great deal of work for charity*. Write down three more sentences from this letter where the writer argues by making clear statements.

2 The words in this statement are in an unusual order:

Selfish and uncaring we are not!

Write the words in a their usual order. Why is the statement more powerful because of the unusual word order?

A **rhetorical question** is a question that does not need an answer. This kind of sentence is used in arguments to get people onto your side:

Are we really meant to believe that all young people are stupid? (The answer is obviously 'no'.)

Surely every one of you agrees that children are naturally kind? (The answer being suggested is 'yes'.)

3 Questions to readers keep them involved in an argument. Write down one rhetorical question used in the letter.

An **imperative** is a sentence structure used to give a suggestion or command. In arguments, imperatives speak directly to the reader.

***Listen** carefully to my words!*

***Don't take** my word for it. **Go and see** for yourself!*

4 Write down one imperative sentence from the third paragraph of the letter, where the writer commands you to do something.

Text

All good argument writing is organised carefully. This letter shows you one way to **structure an argument**.

- The first paragraph is the **thesis**, giving you the writer's point of view.

- Each separate paragraph includes an **argument**. Each argument needs to be supported by **evidence**.

- The last paragraph is the **reiteration**, where the writer repeats the main point of view from the first paragraph.

1 Read the first paragraph of the letter. Write down the words which state the thesis.

2 Read the second and third paragraphs. For each paragraph, note down the writer's argument. Then note down the evidence given for each argument.

3 Read the last paragraph. Write the words which reiterate the writer's thesis. How has the writer avoided repeating the exact words used in the first paragraph?

5 ▷ Planning your own writing

MEDIA RESEARCH

Collect some letters from newspapers and magazines. Not all of them will be giving a point of view. Note down two or three other reasons why people write in.

Choose three letters which argue for or against an opinion. Read them carefully and make notes like this:

Publication	Topic	For/Against	Main points made
Evening Post	Behaviour of teenagers	Against	1 Teenagers are all vandals 2 Teenagers are disrespectful to older people

Write your own letter to the editor of a newspaper or magazine. Argue for or against a point of view.

▶▶ **STARTING POINTS**

- Cars should be banned from city centres.
- More money should be spent on leisure facilities for young people.
- Keeping exotic pets should be illegal.
- Cycle safety-helmets should be compulsory on main roads.

▶▶ **CLUES FOR SUCCESS**

- Begin and end with short paragraphs, to make your thesis clear.
- Keep the tone polite and formal.
- Include facts and statistics to prove you are right.
- Use emotive words to persuade readers to agree with you.
- Use sentence structures that speak directly to readers – clear statements, rhetorical questions and imperatives.

WRITING FRAMES

Choose the writing frame which suits your own point of view.

Sections	Possible phrases		Language features
	For	**Against**	
The thesis State your point of view.	*I was delighted to read …*	*I was concerned/ dismayed/ disgusted to read …*	• clear statement of your opinion
Arguments Give the reasons for your opinion, with evidence.	*I agree because …* *Moreover …* *Of course …* *Some people think …*	*I disagree because …* *What I find unacceptable …* *Some people think …* *However …*	• formal style • emotive words • varied sentence structures • imperatives • rhetorical questions
Reiteration Repeat your thesis.	*I hope other readers will agree that …*	*I hope your readers will join in my protest …*	• sentence structure and words chosen for powerful end

 REDRAFTING AND IMPROVING

Work with a partner. Read each other's letters and see if you can:

- add new ideas or evidence
- change words or sentence structures to make your argument more persuasive
- correct spelling or punctuation mistakes
- You could word process your final version. If you have written a reply to a real letter, you could use e-mail to send it to the paper.

6 ▷ **Looking back**

- **Argument structure** has three parts: the thesis, the arguments and the reiteration.

- **Emotive words** are words chosen to affect the reader's feelings. They may be positive or negative.

- **Rhetorical questions** and **imperatives** (commands) are sentence structures used to speak directly to the reader.

Books are best?

In this unit you will:
- read a speech arguing a point of view
- learn about language used to argue in a debate
- write your own debate speech

▶▶ **Subject links:** *citizenship, ICT*

2 ▶ **Debate speech**

Technology v. books

Mister Chairman, ladies and gentlemen, I am here today to argue against the motion: This house believes that technology will soon replace books.

Ask any young person today for a wish list of things they would like in their room. What do you see there? A TV/VCR, a CD player, a PC with DVD-ROM, a mobile phone: a mass of machinery, a lengthy list of initials.

But books? Nowhere to be seen. Now, this is the kind of 'progress' I really admire. There is nothing to get in the way of fun and relaxation, except for the buzz, bleep and ping of the latest game. If that is 'progress', you can keep it! I hope to convince you that books will never be beaten by technology. Books are better for everyone in many, many ways.

First, you get a huge choice, for books have been around for hundreds of years so there are millions of them. You can learn about the past, or imagine the future. You can read about people and places in any part of the world.

Furthermore, you can learn all the facts you will ever need from books: how to make a perfect pizza, why dinosaurs died out, the causes of the First World War. Different points of view are found in different books, so books help you to think for yourself.

Moreover, books are cheap. Compare the cost of a paperback book with the cost of a computer game. Books are portable and you can take them anywhere. They never break down and they never need new batteries.

Finally, and most important, books educate you: you learn about yourself and about other people; you learn about right and wrong; you also learn how to read and write your own language more skilfully.

People will tell you that television can be educational, with all those history, travel and nature programmes. How many hours of those do you watch every week compared with the soaps and cartoons? Of course, *Neighbours* gives you a great 'education', doesn't it?

On a more serious note, too much technology harms growing children. Sitting staring at a television or computer screen obviously makes you unable to relate to other people. You will never learn anything about friendship and affection from a machine. Psychologists say that watching violence on videos and computer games makes children violent.

Roald Dahl, whose books have entertained and educated all of us, wrote this:

IT ROTS THE SENSES IN YOUR HEAD!
IT KILLS IMAGINATION DEAD!
IT CLOGS AND CLUTTERS UP THE MIND!
IT MAKES A CHILD SO DULL AND BLIND
HIS BRAIN BECOMES AS SOFT AS CHEESE!
HIS POWERS OF THINKING RUST AND FREEZE!
HE CANNOT THINK HE ONLY SEES!

He was criticising television, but what he says is just as true about spending too much time playing computer games, surfing the Internet and sending pointless text messages on mobile phones.

So, I ask you to support imagination, thinking and literacy. Books will never be replaced by technology. Join me in voting against this motion.

3 Key features

The writer or speaker:
- talks directly to the audience, using the pronouns *I* and *you*
- selects only the reasons to support one side of the argument
- uses rhetorical techniques such as irony and exaggeration

- Why was this speech written? What is a debate? What is a motion?
- What is this argument about? Explain the topic clearly and simply in your own words.
- What would be the opinion of the proposer of the motion? What would be the opinion of a person who opposed the motion?

4 ▷ Language skills

Word

Rhetoric, pronounced 'ret-er-ick', is language used to impress and to emphasise a point, especially in a speech. Two rhetorical techniques in this speech are **exaggeration** and **irony**.

Exaggeration is building up a statement to sound more important than it really is.

> *Every minute* of the day, **millions** of pupils are **endlessly** grateful for their education.

❶ Copy these two statements. List the exaggerations from the speech in the right-hand column. Underline the words which make them sound more impressive.

The plain truth	The exaggeration in the speech
1 Books can bring benefits to some people.	
2 A small number of children may be influenced to copy violent behaviour seen on screen.	

❷ In the right-hand column, add two more sentences from the speech which are exaggerated statements. Underline the exaggerated words. Then write the true statements in the left-hand column.

Irony is when you say the opposite of what you mean. In speech, it is often said in a sarcastic tone: *You forgot to bring my books? How clever of you.*

These two statements are examples of words used ironically:

> *This is the kind of 'progress' I really admire.*

> *Neighbours gives you a great 'education'.*

❸ Note down why the ironic words in inverted commas have the opposite of their usual meaning.

Spelling

Stressed vowel sounds give you clues about how a word is spelled. You can hear contrasting sounds in words like *cost*, **book** and *choice*.

Words with **unstressed** vowels are more difficult to spell. *People, travel, educational, skilful* and *that'll* all end with the same 'l' sound, but have five different spellings.

❶ Write the correct spellings of these words ending with the 'l' sound. Use a dictionary for help if you are not sure.

> *pup........, I........, bott........, fin........, dreadf ...., nav........, petr........, they ...., person........, litt........, pist........, tearf........, we........, crack........, tow........*

Sentence

The **colon** (:) is a punctuation mark which shows that more information is to follow in a sentence.

Here is another reason: books are fun!

The **semicolon** (;) is a punctuation mark with a number of uses in long sentences. One is to separate items on a list when the items are longer than single words.

1 Copy this sentence from the speech. It needs a colon and two semicolons, like the example above. Check with the speech that you have used them correctly.

Books educate you you learn about yourself and about other people you learn about right and wrong you also learn how to read and write your own language more skilfully.

Text

Bias is when you only give one side of an argument. A biased argument is one which does not present both sides evenly and fairly. An argument always has at least two sides to it, but in a debate you choose your side and argue only for your point of view.

1 You can show your bias by attacking the other side. Write down the sentences in paragraphs eight and nine of the speech which attack the idea that:

- television is educational
- computers help children to make friends

2 Reread the paragraph where Roald Dahl's poem is quoted. This attacks the other side, without giving any reasons. Write down three criticisms of television made in the poem.

Look at how the speech uses **connectives** (joining words) to introduce new paragraphs and to remind the audience that there are many reasons to agree with the point of view.

3 Note down the four main arguments given in favour of books in the paragraphs beginning with the connectives:

First ... Furthermore ... Moreover ... Finally ...

5 Planning your own writing

Write a debate speech of your own. Remember, you have to take one side and argue against the other side. The motion for debate is: 'This house believes that technology will soon replace books'.

►► STARTING POINTS

You may *propose* the motion. This means you will be presenting arguments for the opposite side from the speech on pages 38–39. Or you may *second* the speaker of the speech and add even more reasons to *oppose* the motion.

Here are some points you might want to include in your arguments.

Proposers of the motion

- Television/Internet can provide more reliable, up-to-date information than books.

- Video and film are better entertainment than books.

- People discuss what they have seen as much as what they read.

- Mobile phones encourage conversation and relationships.

- Technology has shrunk the world and made us more sympathetic to other people.

- Reading is more anti-social than playing computer games.

Opposers of the motion

- Good books last – video and computer games quickly go out of fashion.

- Technology makes us lazy – people expect to have everything provided instead of making their own entertainment.

- Computers, films, videos, etc. are dumbing down culture.

- American influence is damaging the English language.

- Books encourage you to be more selective and critical.

►► CLUES FOR SUCCESS

- Begin with a formal debate opening – state clearly which side you're on.

- Speak directly to your audience: *I* to *you*.

- Give good reasons for your point of view – a mixture of facts and opinions.

- Destroy the opposite point of view.

- Use rhetorical techniques to make points strongly – exaggeration, irony and alliteration.

- Finish by asking your audience to vote *For* or *Against* the motion.

►► REDRAFTING AND IMPROVING

Work in a pair with someone who is on the same side as you. Read your speeches aloud to each other. Check that you:

- begin your speeches clearly

- have a good variety of reasons – facts or opinions

WRITING FRAMES

Use these ideas to help you organise your arguments.

Section	Possible phrases		Language features
	Proposition	Opposition	
Opening	*Madam chairman, ladies and gentlemen, I wish to propose the motion that ...*	*Mister chairman, ladies and gentlemen, I wish to second my colleague in opposing the motion ...*	• formal debating terms
Arguments State the reasons for your point of view	*It is obvious that ...* *Furthermore ...* *Moreover ...* *Of course ...* *Most crucially ...*	*It is clear to all of us that ...* *I would add to my colleague's argument that ...* *A further point for you to consider ...* *Penultimately ...* *Finally ...*	• reasons include facts and opinions • clearly organised in paragraphs • rhetorical techniques: exaggeration, alliteration and irony • accurate use of colons/semicolons on lists
Attack the other side	*Misguided people will tell you ...* *It is quite wrong that ...* *However ...*	*I must disagree with those who support this because ...* *Even if ...* *Otherwise ...*	• rhetoric • expert opinions quoted • rhetorical questions
Appeal for votes	*Join me in support of ... and vote for this motion*	*Give your vote to ... and join my colleague and me in opposing this ridiculous motion*	• short, clear summary – audience told what to do

- use words and sentence structures that include rhetorical techniques
- address your audience directly with questions or commands
- show your bias – destroy the other side's arguments aggressively

6 ▸ Looking back

- **Rhetoric** is language, such as exaggeration or irony, used to emphasise a point in a speech.
- **Colons** and **semicolons** are used to introduce information and to divide up long items on lists.
- **Bias** is the selection of reasons to support only one side of an argument.

Crack the country code

1 ▷ Purpose

In this unit you will:
- read a 'code' which gives advice
- learn how language makes the country code work
- write your own code using the right language

▷▷ **Subject links:** *geography, science, PSHE*

2 ▷ A code giving advice and guidance

The country code

🍃 **Guard against all risks of fire**

🍃 **Fasten all gates**

🍃 **Keep dogs under control**

🍃 **Keep to paths across farmland**

🍃 **Avoid damaging fences, hedges and walls**

Leave no litter

Safeguard water supplies

Protect wildlife, all plants and trees

Go carefully on country roads

Respect the life of the countryside

3 Key features

The writers:

- use imperative verbs to stress what you must do
- make the message clear using short sentences
- choose words carefully to create the right tone

- Why was the country code written?
- Where would you expect to see it displayed?
- Which is the most important sentence in the list? For what reason?

4 Language skills

Word

Imperatives are a form of verb which can be used to give a command

> *Stop!*
> *Keep off the grass.*

In the country code, the words at the beginning of each sentence are imperative verbs.

1 Write down two imperatives which command you *to do* something.

2 Write two imperatives which command you *not to do* something.

If you change the imperative verbs into **requests** or **suggestions**, it makes these sentences less powerful.

> *Keep dogs under control. (command)*

> *Please try to keep your dog under control. (request)*

> *You could keep your dog under control. (suggestion)*

3 Make three columns.

- Write three commands from the country code in the first column.

- Change the words of each sentence into a request. Write them in the second column.

- Change the words of each sentence into a suggestion. Write them in the third column.

Spelling

Words which end with the **suffix -ing** are sometimes called **-ing participles**. If you remove the -ing suffix, you are left with the **root word**. For example:

> *The root word of* bullying *is* bully.
> *The root word of* saying *is* say.

1 Write down the root words of:
commanding, ordering, requesting

There are three different spelling patterns when you add -ing participles to root words.

Some words keep the same spelling as the root word:

> *tell → telling, boss → bossing*

2 Write down three -ing participles with the root word spelled exactly the same.

Some root words change their spelling. Many of these root words end with an e:

> *advise → advising, force → forcing.*

3 Write down three -ing participles where the root word ends with e.

Some words have one letter at the end of the root word which is doubled before -ing:

> *beg → begging; counsel → counselling*

4 Write down three -ing participles where you need to double the final letter of the root word.

Sentence

Simple sentences say just one thing. A simple sentence has one main verb.

You must go now. Main verb is *go.*
Wear these gloves. Main verb is *wear.*

1 How many words are in the shortest sentence in the code? How many words are in the longest sentence? Note down your answers.

2 Why did the writers keep all the sentences short and simple? Note down your reason.

Conjunctions can be used to join two simple sentences, linked in meaning, into a **complex** sentence. These conjunctions give reasons or purposes for an action: *because, in case, so that* ...

*Go now **because** your bus is due in a couple of minutes.*

*Wear these gloves **so that** your hands keep warm.*

1 Add a reason to three of the sentences in the code to explain why we should obey these rules. For example:

*Fasten all gates **in case the animals in the fields escape**.*

Write your three complex sentences.

Text

The **structure** of a text is the way it is put together. Some texts are structured by joining sentences in paragraphs.

Some texts, like this code, are structured as a list of sentences or as a list of single words.

1 Note down a reason why the sentences in this code are organised in a list. Why would it be less clear to readers if the sentences were written one after the other in a paragraph?

We choose a particular **tone** for a text to show our attitude to the reader.

Imperatives may sometimes seem bossy or even impolite: *Do not touch the merchandise!*

Suggestions usually sound more friendly and polite: *It would be better if children under six did not attend.*

2 These are different ways you might ask or tell someone to do something. Which three words from the list below describe the tone used in the country code?

- *begging*
- *advising*
- *forcing*
- *bullying*
- *commanding*
- *ordering*
- *requesting*
- *counselling*
- *telling*
- *bossing*

5 ▷ Planning your own writing

Write a code of your own. Give clear advice to your readers by using the appropriate language and tone.

▷▷ STARTING POINTS

- The Sprogs' Code (guidance for pupils starting secondary school)
- The Family Code (for parents about how to deal with teenagers, or the other way round)
- The Home Safety Code (warnings about hazards in the home)
- The Happy Pet Code (how to care for a new pet)

▷▷ CLUES FOR SUCCESS

- Think carefully about who the code is designed to advise.
- Use a tone that is right for your reader.
- Keep the message simple and clear.
- Ensure you have listed all the important points you need to make.

▷▷ REDRAFTING AND IMPROVING

In groups or pairs look closely at your first drafts. Make suggestions for improving, editing or adding more detail. If you have used a word processor, redrafting is much simpler. Check that:

- the tone you have used is appropriate – pleasant and positive, not too bossy or too weak
- the sentences are clearly expressed
- key points are at the beginning or end of the list
- the layout is easy to follow
- you have made use of headings, bullet points or numbers, clear font and size for text
- any pictures are appropriate and helpful

WRITING FRAMES

Possible phrases

Style a	Style b
Impersonal imperative tone	Recommending tone
Do ...	It is advisable to ...
Avoid ...	You should not ...
Do not ...	Try to avoid ...
Ensure ...	Always ensure that you ...
Remember ...	You should always consider ...
Never ...	Remember that you must ...
Always ...	If you intend to ...
Keep ...	Take great care when ...

Language features
Structure of a & b

- clear, well-organised list of items
- numbers or bullet points

a
- imperative verbs begin sentences
- short, simple sentences
- no reasons

b
- more personal tone – *you*
- longer, complex sentences
- reasons and explanations

6 > Looking back

- **Simple sentences** contain only one clause. They are usually short and get the message across clearly.

- **Imperative verbs** give commands about what you must do, or must not do.

- The **structure** of a text is the way it is organised. A list, with bullet points or numbers, makes the code easy to read. Important items go at the beginning or the end.

How to ...

1 ▶ Purpose

In this unit you will:
- read a Web page that gives advice
- learn how language and layout make advice clear and easy to understand
- write your own 'How to ...' contribution to the Web site

▶▶ **Subject links:** *ICT*

2 ▶ Advice from the internet

A page from the eHow Web site

More than 15,000 How-to solutions

How to: |

| | Do it

Type in what you want to do: e.g. | wash a dog

Home≥Pet Center≥Cats

eHow To Keep Cats From Catching Birds by Karen Bridges

◉ **Steps:**

1. Keep cats indoors at all times.

2. If a cat is accustomed to being outside, put a collar on it with two bells that jingle when the cat moves.

3. Advise neighbors to do the same with their cats, offering to purchase collars and bells for neighbors' cats if appropriate.

4. Keep feeders and birdbaths 10 feet away from foliage where cats can hide.

5. Put chicken wire around feeders and birdbaths to keep cats out.

6. Turn the hose on any stray cats that come into your yard, or chase them away, or otherwise scare them off, repeatedly if necessary.

✱ Tips:

- It is estimated that cats that stay indoors have more than double the lifespan of outdoor cats.

- If a cat injures a bird, contact a licensed bird rehabilitation organization immediately.

⚠ Warnings:

Neighbors with cats are often extremely defensive and resentful toward those who suggest that their felines pose a problem and may react strongly if you spray their cats with water.

View 6 More Tip(s) from Users   Please share your tips with us

Related eHows:
- Attract Goldfinches
- Attract Hummingbirds
- Attract Robins
- Make a Simple Bird Feeder
- Prevent Birds From Flying Into Windows

Related Sites:
- American Bird Conservatory
- Cat Care Society
- Pets.com

🛒 Things You'll Need:

check items you will need
- a cat collar with two bells ☐
- chicken wire ☐
- garden hose ☐

🛒 Shopping

Related Books:
- Cat Care ☐
- Tips 101E ☐

Resources:
- Ask an Expert ☐
- Have it Done ☐

Mail this eHow to a Friend:
Email:

[|]

send

---

3 ⟩ Key features

The writer:
- instructs the reader with short sentences
- gives advice to the reader with longer sentences
- organises her sentences in lists under different sub-headings

- Who wrote this Web page, a cat-lover or a bird-lover? How do you know?
- Which country do you think she lives in? How do you know?
- What is the most effective way to keep cats away from birds?

4 ▷ Language skills

Word

Imperatives are verbs which are used to give instructions or commands.

Chase cats away. (a command to DO something)

Instructions include verbs to tell the reader what to do. Instruction sentences often begin with an imperative.

❶ Steps 1–6 give instructions. List the imperative verbs. (There are three imperatives in Step 6.)

Spelling

American spelling is sometimes different from British spelling.

In America, there is only one way to spell *license*, whether it is a noun or a verb. In Britain, we have two spellings.

I have a driver's licence. (The c at the end shows this is a noun.)

I am licensed to drive. (The s at the end shows this is a verb.)

Other words that follow this rule are *advice/advise, practice/practise*.

A **mnemonic** is a memorable phrase to help you remember something. *Take my advice and see the noun* reminds you of the English spelling rule: *c* is in nouns.

❶ Copy out this mnemonic. Then write your own mnemonic to remind you that *s* is in verbs.

Sentence

A **clause** is a groups of words formed round a verb. A **simple sentence** is just one clause.

*Cats **hunt** birds.*

❶ Which Step is a simple sentence? Write it down and underline the verb.

Clauses can be put together to make longer sentences. A **compound sentence** has two or more clauses joined with a **conjunction** such as *and, or, but.*

*Cats **hunt** birds and sometimes they **injure** them.*

❷ Step 6 is a compound sentence. Write it down and underline all the verbs in this sentence. How many clauses does it have?

A **complex sentence** has two or more clauses, joined together with a word which shows how they are connected in meaning: *because, if, although.*

*Cats hunt birds **because** they enjoy it.*

❸ Step 2 is a complex sentence. Copy it and underline the conjunctions – the words that join the clauses together.

A **comma** is used to divide up clauses in longer sentences.

Commas separate a list of clauses in a compound sentence.

You can bring a coat, or you can come in the car, or you can use an umbrella.

Commas separate the clauses in a complex sentence.

If it is raining, bring your coat.

4 Look at the Steps sentences. You have already copied one compound sentence where commas divide up a list of clauses. Which Step is it? Check that you have used commas correctly.

Text

This Web page shows you a few different ways to organise advice.

An **icon** is a small picture or symbol to represent an idea. The shopping trolley shows that you can buy things.

Sub-headings are used with each icon to divide the Web page into sub-sections.

1 Draw three of the icons from the eHow Web page. Note down how each represents the idea of the sub-heading.

This page shows you two different ways of organising lists: **numbers** and **bullet points**.

Numbers are used for two reasons:

- **progression**: where point one needs to be done before you can move on to point two

1 *Take the teapot.*
2 *Put in two teabags.*

- **priority**: when point one is more important than point two

1 *Put a collar on your cat.*
2 *Advise neighbours to put collars on their cats.*

2 The most important part of the page is the advice in the Steps section. Why is this advice organised with numbers? Why does sentence one come first? Why does sentence six come last? Note down the reasons.

Bullet points are used where the list is **random**, and the order of the items makes no difference.

3 Note down three lists on the eHow Web page which are organised with bullet points. Explain how these lists are different from the list of Steps.

4 Note down which of the following lists would be best organised with numbers and which with bullet points.

- *a reading list*
- *a recipe*
- *a shopping list*
- *how to program your video*
- *things to pack for your holiday*
- *instructions for putting up a shelf*
- *how to eat more healthily*

5 ▷ Planning your own writing

Design your own 'How to ...' contribution to the eHow Web site. Give clear advice and instructions about a subject you know well.

▷▷ STARTING POINTS

- Something personal: how to make lots of friends or how to be a perfect wedding guest
- More advice about pets: how to bath your dog or how to keep your hamster healthy
- Something to make: a recipe for your favourite snack or an idea for a home-made gift
- How to mend or improve something: fix a puncture or upgrade your computer
- Health or beauty tips: hair and nail care or how to deal with spots

▷▷ CLUES FOR SUCCESS

- Organise the advice into sections and lists.
- Use icons, sub-headings, bullet points or numbers to make your message clear.
- Use a variety of sentence structures: some simple imperatives for clear instructions; some longer sentences for tips and warnings.
- Make sure numbered instructions cover all the information needed – and give it in the right order.

▷▷ REDRAFTING AND IMPROVING

Check to see if you can make improvements:

- Add new ideas to some sections.
- Change the order of instructions or the way you have expressed them: vary sentence structures to make ideas clear.
- Improve the layout: use better headings, fonts, bullet points, icons, graphics.
- Correct spelling or punctuation mistakes.

Do your final version on a computer if you can, but you could just as easily design your Web page on paper.

WRITING FRAME

Use the eHow page as a writing frame. Organise your ideas into similar sections. Draft the words first, then think about graphics. Choose new icons, or bullet points if you think they suit your subject. Do you need diagrams to explain your topic clearly?

Section	Possible phrases		Language features
1 The title and author Add a sentence to introduce your topic	*eHow to ...* *It can be a problem when ...*	*by ...*	● use of capital letters
2 The essential advice	Steps: 1 Take ... 2 Put ... 3 Remove ...	or First you should take ... Next you will need to put ... Thirdly, remove ... Penultimately, you must ... Finally, ...	● use of imperatives ● numbered items, or progression shown with words ● varied sentence structures ● commas in longer sentences
3 Extra advice	Tips: It may be helpful to ... For success, you should ... If you mess up, then ...	Warnings: Beware ... Take care not to ... DO/DO NOT ...	● sub-headings ● icons ● colons
4 Extra advice: items and titles	Things you'll need: ● ● ●	Related eHows/ sites/resources/ books: ● ●	● lists ● bullet points

6 ▶ Looking back

- **Imperative verbs** give commands and instructions.
- A **clause** is a group of words formed around a verb. Clauses can be joined together to make long sentences.
- **Sub-headings** with **icons** are used to divide information into sections.
- **Bullet points** list random ideas or items.

Health matters

1 ▶ Purpose

In this unit you will:
- read some advice from a booklet about asthma
- learn how language is chosen to suit readers
- write your own healthcare booklet

▶▶ **Subject links:** *science, physical education*

2 ▶ Healthcare advice

Asthma and exercise

Asthma shouldn't be allowed to rule your life

Nicola, aged 28, is a personnel officer in Nottingham. She was diagnosed as having asthma when she was eight.

'My asthma isn't particularly bad, but I do have hay fever too, so that makes it quite difficult in the summer.

I was very sporty as a child. I loved rounders and athletics, but couldn't run more than 200m because I'd get a bit breathless and I'd always have to keep my reliever inhaler with me. My asthma got worse during exams. I suppose it was because of the stress, but when I started work and began exercising regularly again it seemed to subside and it has gradually got better since then.

These days I know when I need to be careful – between 5 p.m. and 7 p.m. in the evenings, particularly when it's a hot, humid day. I always keep my car windows shut and wear sunglasses when the pollen count is high.

I'm not obsessive about my asthma – you can't be. It's something you have to live with. Asthma shouldn't be allowed to rule your life.'

What brings on an asthma attack?

There are many different asthma triggers and those who are prone to attacks may react to just one or to several. Triggers include: exercise, air pollutants, cigarettes and pollens.

Exercise: Some people with asthma may find exercise improves their condition, but exercising on cold days can affect some people.

What to do: Regular exercise not only keeps your body toned and your weight under control, it can also reduce stress, help you relax and sleep better. It's good for your circulation, helps keep your heart healthy, gives skin a healthy glow – and, above all, it's fun and a good way to meet people who share a similar interest.

On the downside, exercise can also be a trigger for some people with asthma. The best types of exercise for those with asthma are swimming and yoga. Even a brisk, 20-minute walk every day will help. Remember, however, that long spells of exercise are more likely to cause problems than, say, a half-hour fitness class, which gives you rest times between the exercises.

Simple precautions you should take:

- Have one or two puffs of your reliever inhaler about 15 minutes before you start to exercise and keep it with you in case you feel an attack coming on.

- If your chest still gets tight, your asthma may not be under control. Check your peak flow target in your self-management plan and see your doctor in case your treatment needs to be adjusted.

- Long periods of exercise aren't a good idea on cold, dry days or hot, humid days.

- Be particularly careful if you have a cold – your airways will be extra sensitive anyway.

3 ▸ Key features

The writer:
- uses specialist, technical and medical vocabulary
- gives expert advice as well as quoting everyday experience
- organises the advice into different sub-headed sections

- Where would you expect to find a free booklet like this one?
- Who might pick it up and read it: just people who suffer from asthma? Anyone else?
- Find three connections between Nicola's problems and the advice boxes.

4 ▸ Language skills

Word

A **noun phrase** is a group of words which does the job of a noun: the name or label of a thing.

> Exercise gives you **healthy, glowing skin**.

Technical, specialist and scientific language includes noun phrases where two, or more, words are used together.

> beta blocker, preventer inhaler, allergy clinic, step aerobics class, bone thinning disease, peak flow meter

❶ Write down three scientific-sounding noun phrases from the healthcare leaflet. Write simple definitions to explain each phrase.

> Allergy clinic: a place where a doctor tests you to see if you have a bad reaction to foods or chemicals.

Spelling

Many medical words come from ancient Greek, for example *psyche* is the Greek word for mind. There are many words connected with mental health in this **word family**, all beginning with the **letter string** psych- : **psych**iatrist, **psych**ological, **psych**oanalysis.

❶ *Chemist, pharmacist* and *asthma* all have ancient Greek roots. Use a dictionary to write two or three words belonging to each of these three word families, for example *chemical*.

Sentence

A **simple sentence** has just one clause.

> People with asthma can control their condition.

A **complex sentence** is a sentence with two or more clauses, connected by a word which shows how the clauses are joined in meaning. *If, when, because, in case* connect clauses in complex sentences.

> Keep your inhaler with you **in case** you have an attack.

❶ Write down these sentences in two columns. Head the columns **Simple** and **Complex**.

> Smoking is bad for asthma because it can trigger an attack.
>
> Cold weather, wind and humid days can all be asthma triggers.
>
> If you take a brisk, 20-minute walk each day, it will improve your breathing.
>
> Keep away from long grass.
>
> Keep all the windows closed when the pollen count is high.
>
> Exercise is a good way to reduce stress, relax and sleep better.

A **comma** is sometimes used to separate clauses in complex sentences.

> If you are stressed out, exercise is a good way to relax.

Text

When we write something from our own viewpoint, using the pronouns *I* and *me*, we call this writing in the **first person**.

Nicola's case study, where she describes how she copes with asthma, is written in the first person.

> *My asthma isn't particularly bad, but I do have hay fever too ...*

❶ Write two first-person sentences from the leaflet where Nicola explains how she avoids asthma attacks.

The **audience** is the name we give to the people we expect will read our writing or listen to what we say. The advice in the leaflet sounds like an expert talking to the reader. The writer uses the **second-person** pronoun *you*, to talk directly to the audience.

> *Your Doctor will want to know how long you've had your symptoms ...*

❷ Look again at the section of the leaflet sub-headed *Simple precautions you should take*. Write down three sentences where the words *you/your* are used twice or more.

The **structure** of a text is the way it is put together. This text is divided into different sections rather than paragraphs.

❸ Note down how the designers of the leaflet make sections look different from each other on the page. How does the case-study differ from the advice section?

❹ Why are bullet points used in the list of precautions for taking exercise?

5 ▷ Planning your own writing

Write your own healthcare advice leaflet. Give clear advice about how to avoid problems, as well as how to cope with them when they do occur.

⟩⟩ STARTING POINTS

- something you know about from personal experience: living with a food allergy, hay fever, or eczema

- advice for travellers: how to avoid sunburn, holiday tummy, insect bites, etc.

- advice for new parents: nappy rash, teething, choosing a first pair of shoes

- getting fit and staying in good shape – exercise and diet advice

⟩⟩ CLUES FOR SUCCESS

- Organise the expert advice into sections – use sub-headings, or a question-and-answer format.

- Give expert advice – include specialist noun phrases.

- Use text boxes, images, bullet points or numbers to make your message clear.

- Vary your sentence structures.

- Use the second-person audience, *If* ... and *When* ... clauses, and imperatives.

- Include a case study – make sure it reflects the advice given – use first-person and past-tense verbs.

⟩⟩ REDRAFTING AND IMPROVING

In pairs, discuss your leaflets and suggest ways to improve them. See if you can:

- add some extra advice boxes

- vary sentence structures to make ideas clear

- improve ideas in the case study

- present your leaflet with suitable sub-headings, fonts, bullet points, colours and pictures

- correct spelling, especially of technical or specialist words

- correct punctuation, especially commas in complex sentences

- do your final version on a computer – you may find a ready-made template for an A4 leaflet

WRITING FRAME

Use the writing frame to help you organise your ideas into sections.

Section	Possible headings and phrases	Language features
1 Introduce the topic	*What is travel sickness?* *Feelings of dizziness and nausea caused by motion, which confuses the brain ...*	● advice organised with: text boxes sub-headings colour and pictures
2 Problems and solutions	*How can I prevent seasickness?* *You must take two tablets ...* *You can take these up to two hours before ...* **Supposing I still feel sick** *If you continue to feel nauseous, get some fresh air ...* *When you ...* *Always ...* *Never ...*	● technical noun phrases for expert advice ● second-person audience: *you/your* ● commands and suggestions ● varied sentence structures: remember commas in *If .../When ...* sentences
3 Tips and warnings	**Top tips:** ● *Sit at the front.* ● *Open a window.* ● *Avoid reading.* ● *Do ... Don't ... Try to ... etc.*	● lists and bullet points
4 Case study Introduce the sufferer	*James, aged 14, is from London.* *He has suffered from car sickness since ...* *'I was always sick every time we went ...* *Life really changed when my pharmacist suggested a wrist band ...* *These days I love to travel ...* *In the future I might ... '*	● first-person point of view: *I, me, myself* ● chatty, less technical language ● comments linked with the expert advice ● inverted commas round the comments

6 ❯ **Looking back**

- **Noun phrases** are groups of words that do the job of a noun. In advice leaflets, technical, specialist and scientific noun phrases show the writer is an expert.

- **Complex sentences** have two or more clauses joined by a word which shows they are connected in meaning. They can explain the reasons for advice.

- The **first-person** point of view is when you write as *I*; the **second-person** audience is *you*. Use these to speak directly to your reader or listener.

Futures

1 ▶ Purpose

In this unit you will:
- read three different texts about the future
- learn how language is used to forecast events and give advice
- write two kinds of advice for the future

⟩⟩ **Subject links:** *geography, PSHE*

2 ▶ Advice about the future

Today's weather

PRESENTER Good morning. Twenty-six minutes past seven on *GMTV* and time for the weather forecast. If you've been with us, you'll know it's been chucking it down in Dunfermline, but apparently it's all right now. So, what's it going to be like later?

WEATHER FORECASTER It's going to be very nice.

PRESENTER Can I get out in my garden?

WEATHER FORECASTER You will, but don't wear that costume. Do not frighten the neighbours today. *[Laughter from both.]* Now, let's take a look.

Actually it's going to be quite nice here, but out over the Mediterranean, glorious sunshine, if you're flying out that way. Of course, France and Spain as well – lovely holiday weather there – don't forget that suncream.

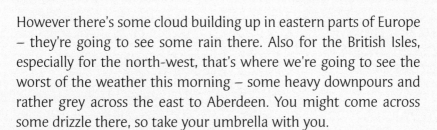

However there's some cloud building up in eastern parts of Europe – they're going to see some rain there. Also for the British Isles, especially for the north-west, that's where we're going to see the worst of the weather this morning – some heavy downpours and rather grey across the east to Aberdeen. You might come across some drizzle there, so take your umbrella with you.

For the northern parts of the country, down to Newcastle, for Ireland, Wales and across to East Anglia and the Home Counties, it will start to brighten up. There may be the odd shower, but it will be light in nature.

Later on, though, we're looking at heavy downpours and it could trigger off some thundery weather much like yesterday, where you in Wales had about one-and-a-half inches of rain. Take care if you're out on the roads in that. Across the south-west, we are currently dominated by low pressure which is where we're getting this rain and there's a possibility of hail in some areas. It will be chillier round these coastal regions where we start seeing this rain later this afternoon. If you've got washing to dry, get it out now, and keep an eye on it later on today.

Here in the south, though, twenty-four degrees, so you'll definitely be able to get out into that garden today. More weather in about half an hour.

Adapted from GMTV *broadcast*

In the stars

ARIES
(Mar 21–April 19)

There will be many changes in your life this week, so it will be best just to let it happen. A short vacation may usher in some of the changes as you meet and become romantically involved with a Leo.

TAURUS
(Apr 20–May 20)

Your spiritual energies run high this week and could draw unusual things to you. Meditate well on your dreams as they carry a message for you.

GEMINI
(May 21–June 21)

Your powers of logical reasoning are not at their highest and you could make a poor choice, so a major purchase may not be in the stars for you this week.

CANCER
(June 22–July 22)

Be aware of a someone close to you who may need your help at this time, could be he is too proud to ask.

LEO
(July 23–Aug 22)

Had a check-up lately? It should be nothing serious, but you should see to it.

VIRGO
(Aug 23–Sept 22)

Demands on your time this week will be heavy and you might find yourself worn out if you don't slip away at least one day for a well-needed break.

LIBRA
(Sept 23–Oct 23)

A friend will be arriving early in the week and you are overjoyed. This person brings welcome news.

SCORPIO
(Oct 24–Nov 21)

Something you have done in the past will come home to roost. Be sure you keep that promise. Honesty is always the best policy as you will find this week.

SAGITTARIUS
(Nov 22–Dec 21)

Friends introduce you to someone you can really get to know, perhaps for the rest of your life.

CAPRICORN
(Dec 22–Jan 19)

Helping loved ones and friends is normal practice in this world, but this week you may be called on to help someone you have often felt hostile towards.

AQUARIUS
(Jan 20–Feb 18)

Do not be impatient to have a certain thing come to pass. Life is short and you should live it one day at a time.

PISCES
(Feb 19–Mar 20)

All the signs are right for a lucky change this week but be sure you weigh all the pros and cons before making the commitment.

Homework hell

I'm getting really stressed about my homework. I feel I have to do it really well to stay in the top sets and sometimes I have to stay up late to finish it. My parents expect a lot of me and I also expect a lot of myself. I've tried talking to my teachers about it but they don't seem to care. How can I cope with the pressure?

Claire, 15, Shropshire

Talk to your parents about the pressures and expectations. They'll speak to your teachers if you need them to. Set yourself a time limit for each piece of homework so that you don't spend all night doing it. The more worked up you get, the more you'll dread it. Remember that it's important to relax and enjoy yourself as well.

School Success

Get the most out of school this year. Here's how:

- Be positive. Having a positive mental attitude is the key to success. You can do anything if you really set your mind to it.

- Be organised. Keeping on top of your work relieves the pressure.

- Keep fit. Doing regular exercise, getting sufficient sleep and eating a balanced diet keeps your energy levels up.

- Have a laugh. It doesn't have to be hard work all the time!

Spot check

My forehead is covered in spots. I've tried loads of creams and spot products, but none of them seem to work and they all cost too much. At the moment my fringe covers them up, but I don't think it suits me and I want to grow it out, but then everyone will be able to see my spots. I'm getting really fed up!

Name & address withheld

If the rest of your face is clear, it sounds like dirt and grease from your fringe could be rubbing onto your forehead causing spots. Wash your hair every or every other day and, when you're not going out, clip your fringe off your face. Cleanse the area morning and evening with a medicated product – creams are effective if you persevere. If this doesn't work you could look at your diet. Too many processed foods can cause spots. Avoid fizzy drinks, try to cut out caffeine and drink more water. If none of these steps work, visit your doctor.

3 ▷ Key features

The writers (or speakers) of all three texts:

- use the second person pronoun *you* to speak directly to the audience
- have a conversational, informal style
- use future tense verb forms

- Where would you expect to see each of these three texts?
- What kind of reader, or listener, would be likely to take notice of each text?
- Which advice would you take most seriously? Why?

4 ▶ Language skills

Word

Time adverbials are words and phrases which tell you when something happens.

Like verbs, they can describe an event from the past, present or future.

- **past**

Yesterday it rained in Wales. I started growing my nails six months ago …

- **present**

At the moment my fringe covers them up. It's all right now.

- **future**

Tomorrow we'll see some sunshine. A friend will be arriving early in the week.

❶ Find five time adverbials from the weather forecast. Write them down in three columns headed **Past**, **Present** and **Future**.

❷ Note down the phrase used most frequently as a time adverbial in the horoscope. Explain why it is used so often.

❸ Note down three time adverbials used in the problem page answers to show that something should be done regularly or continuously.

Spelling

Would, could and *should* are **auxiliary verbs.** These are verb forms we put before the main verb to change its meaning.

The sun shines. (*Shines* is the main verb.)

The sun could shine later. (*Shine* is still the main verb. *Could* is an auxiliary verb.)

❶ Make sure you can spell the *-ould* letter string correctly. Make up a mnemonic to help you remember the order of the letters, for example a memorable phrase like: **O**ld **U**mbrellas **L**eak **D**rips.

Sentence

The **tense** of a verb is the form that tells us when something happens. Verbs can be in:

the **past** tense: *It **rained** heavily in Wales*.

the **present** tense: *It **is raining** in Dunfermline*.

the **future** tense: *It **will rain** heavily in the south-west*.

A writer sometimes uses more than one verb tense in a text. In a weather forecast the presenter compares yesterday's weather with today's and tells you what to expect later on, so you will find verbs in past, present and future forms. All of these extracts use more than one verb tense. Advice usually tells you how you should behave in the future, so you will find more future tense verbs in advice texts than in some other kinds of writing.

❶ Write out these sentences and underline the verbs. Write *past*, *present* or *future* at the end of each sentence.

> *There will be many changes in your life this week.*
>
> *Honesty is always the best policy.*
>
> *Something you have done in the past will come home to roost.*
>
> *I've tried talking to my teachers.*
>
> *Too many processed foods can cause spots.*
>
> *I'm getting stressed out about my homework.*

It's going to be very nice.

We are dominated by low pressure.

It's been chucking it down in Dunfermline.

Modal verbs are auxiliary verbs which can be used to suggest possible events or actions rather than definite ones. *Might, ought, can, may, would* and *should* are all modal verbs.

> *You **might need** an umbrella if the rain comes back.*
>
> *People **ought to be** more sensitive about the feelings of others.*

❷ Write down two sentences from each of the three texts with different modal verbs. Underline the modal verb and the main verb, like this:

> *There <u>may be</u> the odd shower later.*

❸ Which of the texts uses modal verbs most frequently? Write down a reason for this.

Text

Verbs can be in the **first person**, with the pronouns *I* or *we*, in the **second person**, *you*, or in the **third person**, *he, she, it* or *they*. Writers of texts like these use **second-person** verbs, with the pronoun *you*, to give advice to the reader personally.

> *The more worked up* **you get**, *the more* **you'll dread** *it.*

Advice also includes many **imperatives**, suggestions or commands to the reader to do something.

> *You could come across drizzle, so* **take** *your umbrella.*

> **Wash** *your hair every day ...*

> **Slip** *away ... and* **take** *a well-needed break.*

❶ Find a sentence in the second person from each text. Write these down.

❷ Write a sentence from the horoscope where the writer asks the reader a direct question.

❸ Write an imperative sentence from each text.

A **colloquial style** of writing is one which is closer to everyday, informal speech. Advice is usually given in a chatty, colloquial style. This makes it sound as if the writer is talking to the reader like a friend. In these sentences, the bold words create a colloquial style.

> *It'll be* **chillier** *in coastal regions where we start seeing this rain.*

> *You might find yourself* **worn out** *if* **you don't slip** *away one day.*

> *The more* **worked up** *you get, the more* **you'll** *dread it.*

❶ Write down another sentence with some colloquial words and phrases from each of the three texts. Underline the colloquial words in each sentence.

To contrast with this chatty style, you will notice some **formal, specialist vocabulary**. This shows that the writer, or speaker is an expert who gives advice you can trust.

❷ Write down these sentences and underline the specialist words.

> *We are currently dominated by low pressure across the south-west ...*

> *Your spiritual energies run high this week ... Meditate well on your dreams.*

> *Cleanse the area morning and evening with a medicated product ...*

5 ▷ Planning your own writing

Write your own magazine page. Include two different kinds of advice about the future for your readers.

▷▷ STARTING POINTS

- a hobby magazine for younger readers with a letters page and an article giving tips about improving your skills at football, or computer games
- a fishing or sailing magazine with a weather outlook and advice replying to readers' questions
- a young women's magazine with problem page and horoscope column
- a script for a television 'magazine' programme to include a weather forecast and a phone-in where viewers ask for cookery or gardening advice

▷▷ CLUES FOR SUCCESS

- Give personal advice to the reader using second-person verbs and imperatives.
- Give expert advice by including specialist words and phrases.
- Vary sentence structures with time adverbials and different verb tenses.
- Organise advice into sections – sub-headings, or a question-and-answer format.
- Use text boxes and bullet points if they make your advice more clear.

▷▷ REDRAFTING AND IMPROVING

Check your two pieces of writing to make sure:

- the layout and images suit the text and make it easy to read
- the sentence structures use a variety of tenses, and include modal verbs and time adverbials
- the style is a convincing mixture of chatty phrases and technical expressions
- the spelling and punctuation are accurate

Do your final version on a computer if you can.

WRITING FRAMES

Advice text	Weather forecast	Horoscope	Problem page
Usual layout	in sections according to areas of the country or time of day	twelve sections – one for each sign of the zodiac subheadings may be signs, dates or both	several letters about similar problems, each followed by expert's reply
Images	weather map with symbols for sun, cloud, rain, etc	drawings of zodiac symbols	may include photos to illustrate one letter
Language features	• use of *we* as well as *you* • chatty advice about how to cope • specialist weather terms give information • past, present and future tense verbs and time adverbials	• imperative verbs and questions involve the reader • use of astrological specialist words • many modal verbs; past, present and future tense verbs and time adverbials	• letters written in first person, *I* • letters often end with a question • answers written in second person, *you* • Many imperative verbs • medical or counselling specialist words • time adverbials show continuous and ongoing actions

6 ▷ Looking back

- **Time adverbials** are words and phrases which tell you when events happen.

- **Modal verbs** are auxiliary verbs which can express future possibilities, when the writer cannot be definite about events, for example in a horoscope.

- **Second-person verbs** involve the reader by speaking personally to you.

- **Colloquial style** sounds like everyday conversation. It makes the writer of an advice text seem like a friend. **Specialist words** make the writer sound like an expert you can trust.

I have a dream

1 ## Purpose

In this unit you will:
- read two persuasive speeches and a song lyric
- learn how language is used to stir listeners into action
- write your own 'Dream for the Future' speech

» **Subject links:** *history, English literature, drama, citizenship*

2 ## Persuasive speeches

I have a dream

Martin Luther King gave one of the most famous speeches of the twentieth century to a civil rights march in Washington DC in 1963.

I say to you, my friends, that even though we must face the difficulties of today and tomorrow, I still have a dream that one day this nation will rise up and live out the true meaning of its creed: 'We hold these truths to be self-evident; that all men are
5 created equal.'

I have a dream that one day on the red hills of Georgia the sons of former slaves and the sons of former slaveowners will be able to sit down together at the table of brotherhood.

I have a dream that one day even the state of Mississippi, a state
10 sweltering with the heat of injustice, sweltering with the heat of oppression, will be transformed into an oasis of freedom and justice.

I have a dream that my four little children will one day live in a nation where they will not be judged by the colour of their skin but by the content of their character.

15 I have a dream today!

I have a dream that one day the glory of the Lord will be revealed and all flesh shall see it together.

This is our hope. This is the faith that I go back to the South with. With this faith we will be able to work together, to pray together, to
20 struggle together, to go to jail together, to stand up for freedom together, knowing that we will be free one day.

This will be when all of God's children will be able to sing with new meaning:

    'My country 'tis of thee
25   Sweet land of liberty,
    Of thee I sing:
    Land of where my fathers died,
    Land of the pilgrims' pride
    From every mountainside
30   Let freedom ring.'

When we let freedom ring, when we let it ring from every village and every hamlet, from every state and every city, we will be able to speed up that day when all of God's children, black men and white men, Jews and Gentiles, Protestants and Catholics, will be able to
35 join hands and sing in the words of the old Negro spiritual, 'Free at last! Thank God Almighty, we are free at last!'

Martin Luther King

Animal Farm

George Orwell's novel, Animal Farm, *tells the story of the Russian Revolution by a parallel tale of animals rebelling against human beings. Old Major, a pig, begins the story with this speech to the other animals.*

Comrades, you have heard already about the strange dream that I had last night. But I will come to the dream later. I have something else to say first. I do not think, comrades, that I shall be with you for many months longer, and before I die, I feel it my duty
5 to pass on to you such wisdom as I have acquired.

Now, comrades, what is the nature of this life of ours? Let us face it: our lives are miserable, laborious, and short. We are born, we are given just so much food as will keep the breath in our bodies, and those of us who are capable of it are forced to work to the last atom of our strength; and
10 the very instant that our usefulness has come to an end we are

slaughtered with hideous cruelty. No animal in England knows the meaning of happiness or leisure after he is a year old. No animal in England is free. The life of an animal is misery and slavery: that is the plain truth.

15 Is it not crystal clear, then, comrades, that all the evils of this life of ours spring from the tyranny of human beings? Only get rid of Man, and the produce of our labour would be our own. Almost overnight we could become rich and free. What then must we do? Why, work night and day, body and soul, for the overthrow of the human race! That is my message
20 to you, comrades: Rebellion! I do not know when that Rebellion will come, it might be in a week or in a hundred years, but I know, as surely as I see this straw beneath my feet, that sooner or later justice will be done.

And now, comrades, I will tell you about my dream of last night ... It was a dream of the earth as it will be when Man has vanished. It reminded
25 me of something that I had long forgotten. Last night, it came back to me in my dream. And what is more, the words of the song also came back. I will sing you that song now, comrades.

Soon or late the day is coming,
Tyrant Man shall be o'erthrown,
30 And the fruitful fields of England
Shall be trod by beasts alone.

Rings shall vanish from our noses,
And the harness from our back,
Bit and spur shall rust forever,
35 Cruel whips no more shall crack.

Bright will shine the fields of England,
Purer shall its waters be,
Sweeter yet shall blow its breezes
On the day that sets us free.

40 Beasts of England, beasts of Ireland,
Beasts of every land and clime,
Hearken well and spread my tidings
Of the golden future time.

George Orwell

Imagine

This song lyric was recorded by John Lennon in 1971. His ideas and beliefs were influenced by protests against America at war in Vietnam in the1960s. He had spent some time in India learning about Hinduism and Buddhism. The song is about world peace.

IMAGINE

Imagine there's no heaven
It's easy if you try
No hell below us
Above us only sky
Imagine all the people
Living for today ...

Imagine there's no countries
It isn't hard to do
Nothing to kill or die for
And no religion too
Imagine all the people

Living life in peace ...
Imagine no possessions
I wonder if you can
No need for greed or hunger
A brotherhood of man
Imagine all the people
Sharing all the world ...

You may say I'm a dreamer
But I'm not the only one
I hope someday you'll join us
And the world will be as one

John Lennon

3 > Key features

The speakers and writers:

- choose powerful vocabulary and use many contrasting words
- begin and end with inspiring words
- use repetition to influence their listeners

- Who makes each of the speeches? Who is the audience of each one?
- What similarity is there in the words of the speeches?
- What action does each speaker want listeners to take after hearing these speeches?

4 Language skills

Word

An **antonym** is a word which has the opposite meaning to another word:

slavery/freedom
denied/allowed

These texts place antonyms together so that the contrast makes an impact on listeners. The words compare an unbearable present with a better future.

1 Write down the sentence from Martin Luther King's speech, on page 72, that begins:

I have a dream that one day even the state of Mississippi...

Oasis contrasts with the words *sweltering heat*. Write down the words which are antonyms of *injustice* and *oppression*.

2 Copy the chart and complete the second column with these words from John Lennon's 'Imagine':

- *above us only sky*
- *world will be as one*
- *peace*
- *sharing*
- *brotherhood of man*

Now: things that divide people	Future: things that unite people
kill/die	
greed/hunger	
possessions	
countries	
heaven/hell	

Spelling

Abstract nouns are labels given to things we cannot touch, such as emotions or ideas. States of suffering and happiness are named by abstract nouns, so there are examples in these speeches: *freedom, brotherhood, misery*.

The suffixes *-ty* or *-ity* are often used to turn an adjective into an abstract noun. The **root** adjective is the word before any suffix is added: *safe* becomes *safety*, *sensitive* becomes *sensitivity*.

The root adjective may change its spelling. It may lose a letter: *sensitive* loses its final *e*.

Sometimes one or more letters change: *poor* becomes *poverty*.

1 Note down the abstract nouns in the speeches linked with these adjectives. The first one is done for you

prosperous – prosperity
liberated –
cruel –

2 Make these adjectives into abstract nouns. The first one is done for you. These nouns are not in the speeches or song, so you might need to use a dictionary to check spelling.

one – unity
equal, noble, humble, brief, social

Sentence

Repetition is used in speeches to emphasise important points. Martin Luther King repeats the words *I have a dream that one day ...* to begin four sentences in the first half of his speech

❶ Note down the point that King gets across with these words. How many times are they repeated throughout the whole speech?

❷ Note down three separate words repeated in the second half of King's speech. How many times is each of these words used? What point is emphasised by their repetition?

The rule of three is a technique where three phrases, or even three sentences, similar in structure and meaning, are repeated. Speakers do this to make a dramatic point.

Three phrases:

All of God's children ...
*... **black men and white men**,*   *(1)*
*... **Jews and Gentiles**,*   *(2)*
*... **Protestants and Catholics** ...* *(3)*
... will be able to join hands ...

❸ Write down this sentence from another part of Martin Luther King's speech and underline the repeated rule of three phrases, like the examples above.

> *I have a dream that one day ... every hill and mountain shall be made low, the rough places shall be made plain, and the crooked places shall be made straight and the glory of the Lord shall be revealed...*

A **simple sentence** is one which contains only one clause. Simple sentences can be very powerful. An example is Martin Luther King's *I have a dream today.* This contrasts with the long sentences leading up to it

❹ Write down one powerful, simple sentence from the second paragraph of Old Major's speech.

Text

Beginnings and endings of speeches need to be especially powerful. The beginning must grab listeners' attention. Many speakers stress that they and their audience are on the same side.

❶ Note down the name that Martin Luther King calls his listeners and the name that Old Major keeps repeating. In pairs, discuss the difference between these two names. Decide what kind of speech would be likely to use each one, and why:

The ending of a speech should inspire the listeners to do something.

❷ Note down a similarity between Old Major's ending and Martin Luther King's. What are they both encouraging listeners to do?

❸ Which words at the end of John Lennon's song are similar to King's final sentence?

5 ▶ Planning your own writing

Write a persuasive speech of your own. Try to persuade your listeners to support you in the struggle to make a dream come true

▶▶ STARTING POINTS

I have a dream that one day …

- there will be no more poverty or hunger in the world

- all the people of the world will live in peace

- young people will have equal rights with adults

- schools will be closed and pupils will be set free

▶▶ CLUES FOR SUCCESS

- Begin by gaining listeners' attention and trust.

- Speak directly to your listeners – use nouns *friends, comrades, brothers and sisters* – and use first- and second-person words: *I, you, we, our.*

- Contrast the bad things of the past with the dream of the future: use emotive words as antonyms.

- Use repetition and the rule of three to make points strongly.

- Finish with a powerful call into action

▶▶ REDRAFTING AND IMPROVING

Work in pairs. Read your speeches aloud to each other. Check that you:

- begin your speeches in a way that grabs listeners' attention

- use positive and negative emotive words to affect listeners' feelings

- contrast details of the 'bad old life' with details of a 'perfect future'

- address your audience directly – add questions or imperatives

- end with a powerful call to action

WRITING FRAMES

Use these ideas to help you organise your speech.

Section	Possible phrases	Language features
Beginning	*Brothers and sisters, imagine there's no …* *I have a dream my trusted friends …*	• listeners called by a name that gains their trust
Emphasise the bad experiences	*Fifty years ago English children …* *Today/now we all deplore …* *No …, no … , no … and that is the plain truth.* *Is it not crystal clear that all of this is caused by …?* *I have a dream today!*	• emotive words get listeners involved and cause anger • repetition, rule of three, • varied sentence structures: imperatives (orders) questions • short, simple sentences for emphasis
Describe the changes in the future	*What, then, must we do?* *This is our hope …* *In a week or in a hundred years …* *A golden time of peace and prosperity …*	• use of: I, you, we, our • positive emotive words for feelings of hope and joy • include imperatives and questions
Ending	*Follow your spirit …* *Join us …* *Let freedom ring …*	• short, rousing last sentence, calling listeners to action • an imperative

6 ▷ **Looking back**

- **Antonyms** are words with opposite meanings.
- **Repetition** and the **rule of three** are used to emphasise a point and to build up to a climax in a speech.
- **Beginnings and endings** of persuasive speeches need to be particularly powerful.

Glossary

Abstract noun The label we give to things we cannot touch, e.g feelings or ideas.

Active/passive verbs Two ways of describing an action. Active verbs focus on the person doing the action. Passive verbs focus on the action.

Adjective A word used to describe someone or something.

Adverb A word used to give more information about a verb.

Alliteration The repetition of the initial sound of several words.

Antonym A word which has the opposite meaning to another word.

Apostrophe A punctuation mark (') used to show where a letter has been missed out.

Audience The people we expect to read our writing.

Auxiliary verb A verb form we put before the main verb.

Clause A group of words formed round a verb. A **simple sentence** is just one clause. A **complex sentence** and a **compound sentence** have two or more clauses.

Colloquial style Informal, everyday speech and writing.

Colon A punctuation mark (:) which shows that there is something else to follow in the sentence.

Comma A punctuation mark (,) used to break up sentences.

Compound word Two, or more, words joined into one like *blackbird*.

Connective A word, or phrase, which joins parts of a sentence, or joins sentences into paragraphs, or joins paragraphs in a text.

Emotive word A word chosen to have an effect on readers' feelings.

Exaggeration When something sounds more important than it really is.

First person Writing from your own viewpoint, using the pronouns *I* or *we*.

Homophones Words which sound the same, but have a different spelling and meaning.

Icon A small picture or symbol to represent an idea.

Imperative A form of verb or a sentence structure used to give a command.

Informal writing imitates speech.

Irony When you say or write the opposite of what you mean, in a sarcastic tone.

Jargon Words used by people who share the same job or interest.

Modal verbs Auxiliary verbs used to suggest possible events or actions rather than definite ones.

Neologism A newly invented word.

Noun The name or label of a thing.

Play on words Use of a word with more than one meaning, for a humorous effect.

Pronoun A word used instead of a noun.

Rhetoric Language used to impress and to emphasise a point, especially in a speech.

Rhetorical question A question that does not need an answer.

Second person When the pronoun *you* is used, this is called the second person of the verb.

Semicolon A punctuation mark (;) used in longer sentences.

Subheadings Divide a text into shorter sections.

Synonym A word which means the same as another word.

Tense The form of a verb that tells us when something happens, either in the past, the present or the future